Concord
Massachusetts

in History, Literature and the Arts

Ron McAdow

PHP

Personal History Press
Lincoln, Massachusetts

ISBN: 979-8-9877537-0-5

The author acknowledges the assistance of John Netzer, manager of the Concord Bookshop, who suggested the need for a collection of pictures of Concord. The text benefited from suggestions of readers Barbara Forman, Anke Voss, and Betsy Stokey. Thank you to the Concord Museum and the Concord Art Association for permitting use of their images, and to the Concord Free Public Library for being such a rich source of information.

Interior illustrations are photographs by the author unless otherwise attributed.

The front cover illustration is a composite from four images. The busts, on exhibit at the Concord Free Public Library, are of Louisa May Alcott and Ralph Waldo Emerson. Alcott is by Walton Ricketson; Emerson is by Daniel Chester French. The diorama of the Old Manse by Louise Stimson is also on display at the library. The action at the bridge is from a photograph of a diorama at the Concord Museum, more fully shown and attributed on page seven.

≈

Ron McAdow's previous non-fiction books include *Concord Village* and *Emerson's Nature*. His novels are *Ike* and *The Grove of Hollow Trees*.

PHP

Personal History Press
Lincoln, Massachusetts

The Minuteman
1874
Daniel Chester French.

Welcome to Concord!

America's struggle for independence began with an exchange of musketry witnessed by Concord's minister, who had encouraged his parishioners to rise against the British. A century later, sculptor Daniel Chester French's "Minuteman" was unveiled, its pedestal inscribed with words by the minister's grandson, Ralph Waldo Emerson.

> By the rude bridge that arched the flood,
> Their flag to April's breeze unfurled,
> Here once the embattled farmers stood
> And fired the shot heard round the world.

The skirmish at the bridge, the philosophic writer, and the famous sculptor stand as emblems of Concord's role in American history, literature, and the arts. Concord's significance extends well beyond its icons, as has been documented by many scholars. This small volume is intended as an introduction to this storied New England town and its most prominent sources of interest.

Fluted projectile point, about 11,000 years before present.

Concord Museum Collection

Gift of Mrs. Adams Tolman; 1990.26.332.

History

People have lived in the area we call Concord for millenia, stretching back to the end of the last ice age. The stone point shown above, found in this town, was made about 11,000 years ago. The local population of hunter-gatherers rose and fell over the centuries.

Agriculture has been practiced here for about a thousand years. Its arrival from the southwest inaugurated a way of life that lasted until contact with Europeans in the early 1600s. Epidemics of Old World diseases severely reduced the native population.

When the English arrived, four Eastern Algonquian-speaking tribes lived in what became eastern Massachusetts. Concord lies in the boundary area among three of these groups: the Nipmuck, Pawtucket, and Massachusetts.

English Puritan immigrants established Boston and Watertown in 1630. Prime farmland with access to salt marsh hay was quickly allocated and the settlers looked westward for meadowland. The flat margin of the Concord River, fertile with silts from glacial lakes, was rich in native grasses needed to feed the English cattle.

Concord, the Puritan settler's first inland town, was established in 1635. Two years later leaders of the indigenous people met with the newcomers, accepted gifts or payments, and signed a document that the English considered title to thirty-six square miles of land. Concord's geographical dimensions shrank over time as outlying areas were incorporated into separate towns.

Concord's early inter-town roads led to adjacent Puritan settlements: Watertown to the east, Sudbury to the south, Lancaster to the west, and Billerica to the north. Because Concord was centrally located with respect to other eastern Massachusetts towns, it became a commercial and political center rather early in the colonial period. Most families farmed for subsistence and pursued various crafts as cash-generating side-livelihoods, including small-scale mills for sawing logs and grinding grain.

Concord's first meetinghouse was on a neighboring site. The second was built here in 1673. This is the fourth meetinghouse, rebuilt in 1901, after a fire, from the design used in 1841.

Reverend William Emerson was the minister at Concord's First Parish Church at the start of the War for Independence. In 1774 the Massachusetts Provincial Congress met here to plan resistance, with John Hancock presiding.

After the French and Indian War (1754–1763) tension over governance and taxation stressed the colonies' relationship with Britain. In response to the Boston Tea Party, Parliament had passed the "Intolerable Acts" closing the port of Boston, suspending the Massachusetts legislature, and placing the colony under the rule of General Gage, who occupied Boston with British troops. The general's authority was effective only within the city; the rest of the colony formed its own government. Companies of militia began training in towns throughout New England. Militant colonial planning meetings took place in Concord, and munitions were stored here.

Concord, along with Lexington and Lincoln, saw the earliest violence in America's War for Independence. On the night of April 18, 1775, British troops were dispatched from Boston to destroy military supplies in Concord. When the British troop movement began, William Dawes and Paul Revere rode west to alert the countryside. Revere was stopped by a British patrol, but Dr. Samuel Prescott carried the warning to Concord. Rev. William Emerson, whose house became known as the Old Manse, (see page 10) recorded the sequel in his diary:

> 1775. 19 April. This morning, between one and two o'clock, we were alarmed by the ringing of the bell, and upon examination found that the troops, to the number of eight hundred, had

Reconstruction of the Old North Bridge as it looked in the 1890s.

The Barrett Farm was the deepest penetration by British troops on their march into Massachusetts's interior on April 19, 1775. The detachment that searched the farm for military supplies had crossed the North Bridge and marched two more miles west to reach Barrett's. The fight at the bridge took place before they returned.

This was the home of Concord militia Colonel James Barrett (1710 – 1779) and his family.

stolen their march from Boston, in boats and barges, from the bottom of the Common over to a point in Cambridge, and were at the Lexington meeting-house half an hour before sunrise, where they had fired upon a body of our men and, as we afterward heard, had killed several. This intelligence was brought us first by Dr. Samuel Prescott, who narrowly escaped the guard that were sent before on horses, purposely to prevent all posts and messengers from giving us timely information. He, by the help of a very fleet horse, crossing several walls and fences, arrived at Concord at the time above.

Some were for making a stand, notwithstanding the superiority of their number: but others, more prudent, thought best to retreat, till our strength should be equal to the enemy's, by recruits from neighboring towns that were continually coming in to our assistance. Accordingly we retreated over the bridge. The troops came into the town; set fire to several carriages for the artillery, destroyed sixty barrels of flour, rifled several houses, took possession of the town-house, destroyed five hundred pounds of balls, set a guard of a hundred men at the North Bridge, and sent up a party to the house of Col. Barrett, where they were in expectation of finding a quantity of warlike stores. But these were happily secured, just before their arrival, by transportation into the woods and other by-places.

In the mean time, the guard set by the enemy to secure the posts at the North Bridge were alarmed by the approach of our people, who were now advancing

Plate II A View of the Town of Concorde

1. Companies of the Regulars marching into Concord.
2. Companies of Regulars drawn up in order.
3. A Detachment destroying the Provincial Stores.
4 & 5 Colonel Smith & Major Pitcairn viewing the Provincials who were mustering on an East Hill in Concord.
6. The Townhouse. 7. The Meetinghouse.

A. Doolittle Sculp!

"The British Army in Concord, April 19, 1775. Plate II A view of the town of Concord."

Amos Dootlittle's engravings are the only pictorial record by a contemporary American of the battle that started the American Revolution. In the days after the alarm, Doolittle, a young silversmith of New Haven, Connecticut, had marched with his militia unit to assist in the siege of Boston. He took leave from his unit to visit Lexington and Concord with his artistic friend Ralph Earl. By interviewing participants and witnesses, they formed a detailed understanding of what had taken place. Based on his friend's drawings and what he had learned, Doolittle engraved four copper plates. He advertised prints for sale the following December.

Of the three British soldiers killed at the North Bridge, two lie buried here, near where they fell.

American militia crossed open fields to intercept and assault the British column as it returned to Boston.

Meriam House, in Concord, where the rolling attack began. It is at the west end of the April 19 "battle road."

Facing page: A diorama at the Concord Museum: "Model of the Fight at the Old North Bridge" by Samuel Guernsey and Theodore Pitman, 1930.

with special orders not to fire upon the troops unless fired upon. These orders were so punctually observed, that we received the fire of the enemy in three several and separate discharge of their pieces before it was returned by our commanding officer. The firing then soon became general for several minutes, in which skirmish two were killed on each side and several of the enemy wounded.

A party of our men took the back way, through the Great Fields, into the east quarter, and had placed themselves to advantage, lying in ambush behind walls, fences, and buildings, ready to fire upon the enemy on their retreat.

Colonial militia streamed toward Concord from all directions. By the time the scarlet-clad column began its withdrawal toward Boston, it was surrounded by hostile forces, enraged but disorganized. For the most part the Americans were kept out of musket range of the column by British flankers, but where militia gained positions near the road they took a heavy toll.

By the time the British reached Charlestown 73 had died and 174 were wounded. The colonials suffered 49 dead and 40 wounded. The exhausted British soldiers were ferried across the river and collapsed into Boston, and the Americans laid siege to the city. The following year, George Washington and the Continental Army forced the British to evacuate with cannons captured at Fort Ticonderoga.

Ralph Waldo Emerson, 1803-1882.

from *Concord* by George Bartlett, 1895

The Emerson House, on Cambridge Turnpike in Concord, looks much the same today. Tours are available mid-April to mid-October.

Writers

The American Revolution was followed by the Industrial Revolution. Although central Concord's small supply of water energy, Mill Brook, had been grinding grain and powering other tasks since the first year of settlement, large-scale industry had to be sited elsewhere, because the town was on a flat river, not at a fall. The earliest and largest textile mills in Massachusetts were built at Waltham, Lowell, and Lawrence. Concord remained bucolic—an appealing environment for nature-loving Transcendentalists.

Ralph Waldo Emerson was born in Boston. His father, a successful Unitarian minister, died young. The widow and her family received support from and often lodged with her father-in-law at what has long been called the Old Manse in Concord.

The younger Emerson followed in the profession of his forebears, accepted a prestigious pulpit in Boston, and married a beautiful girl. But it all fell apart. His bride died of tuberculosis at nineteen, his rejection of traditional sacraments led him to leave his congregation, and his own health was troubled. In 1833, hoping to recover his spirits and his health, Emerson sailed for Europe. The thoughts, experiences, and conversations he had there sent him home with the germ of his first book, *Nature*, and a desire to live in

Bronson Alcott

Amos Bronson Alcott, (1799 – 1888) was a native of Connecticut. He and his wife, Abby May Alcott, and his four daughters lived in Concord for many years. Bronson was a leader in the Transcendental movement.

Dove Cottage today.

The Alcotts rented this house, also known as "The Dovecote," for their initial stay in Concord. When they returned, they lived first in Hillside, later in Orchard House and finally in the Thoreau-Alcott House on Main Street.

the country. He considered the Berkshires, but Concord had strong attractions. It was within stagecoach reach of towns and cities where he could preach and lecture. His brother Charles was in love with a Concord woman and intended to live there with her. And Waldo's boyhood experiences in the town's woods and fields were alive in his mind and imagination. He moved to the Manse (which became the "Old Manse" when Hawthorne called it that; see page 10) and began to write his book. He remarried, bought the house on Cambridge Turnpike still owned by his descendants, and published *Nature*. He became America's first public intellectual.

An educator and philosopher named Bronson Alcott drew the attention of Emerson, who urged the Alcotts to move to Concord. In 1840, they did so, renting a house they called Dove Cottage. Like Emerson, Bronson Alcott was a philosophical idealist, but his talents lay in education rather than in writing or public speaking. The Alcotts left Concord in 1843 to lead a short-lived utopian community called Fruitlands, in the town of Harvard, sixteen miles northwest of Concord. Bronson Alcott was kind and charismatic but catastrophically impractical, as the Fruitlands experiment demonstrated.

Meanwhile, an aspiring novelist had arrived. Nathanael Hawthorne rented the

From *Mosses from an Old Manse* by Nathaniel Hawthorne

The glimmering shadows that lay half asleep between the door of the house and the public highway were a kind of spiritual medium seen through which the edifice had not quite the aspect of belonging to the material world.

From these quiet windows the figures of passing travelers look too remote and dim to disturb the sense of privacy.

The boughs over my head seemed shadowy with solemn thoughts as well as with rustling leaves.

I took shame to myself for having been so long a writer of idle stories, and ventured to hope that wisdom would descend upon me with the falling leaves of the avenue, and that I should light upon an intellectual treasure in the Old Manse.

There was in the rear of the house the most delightful little nook of a study that ever offered its snug seclusion to a scholar. It was here that Emerson wrote *Nature*, for he was then an inhabitant of the manse.

People that had lighted on a new thought or a thought that they fancied new came to Emerson, as the finder of a glittering gem hastens to a lapidary to ascertain its quality and value. It was good to meet him in the wood-paths, or sometimes in our avenue, with that pure intellectual gleam diffused about his presence like the garment of a shining one, and he so quiet, so simple, so without pretension, encountering each man alive as if expecting to receive more than he could impart.

Bronson Alcott's drawing of Hillside. When the Hawthornes bought it, they renamed The Wayside.

Old Manse and lived there for the first three years of his marriage to Sophia, the artist among the distinguished Peabody sisters. Using the diamond in her new ring, Sophia inscribed the windows with words that can be read by visitors today. Hawthorne wrote about the old house and its town in *Mosses from an Old Manse*. Nathaniel and Sophia returned to their native Salem for a few years, then lived for a time in the Berkshires, but both they and the Alcotts returned to Concord.

In 1845, the Alcotts moved to a house on Lexington Road they called Hillside. When Bronson's daughter Louisa May wrote *Little Women*, she set it during the Civil War, but the real-life activities of the Alcott sisters took place during their earlier years at Hillside. The Hawthornes subsequently purchased Hillside and re-named it The Wayside.

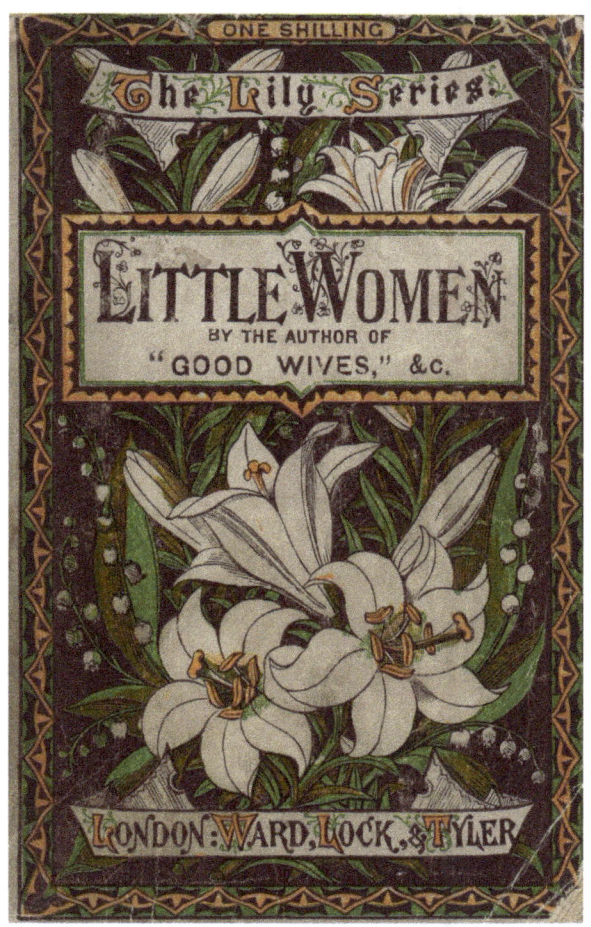

English edition, 1878 Wikimedia Commons

Detroit Publishing Company. Wikimedia Commons

The Wayside in 1901. The tower to the left of the chimney was a Hawthorne addition.

Visitor's Memorial. The site of Thoreau's Hut at Lake Walden.

Photo from *Concord* by George Bartlett, 1895

Top: replica of the cabin Thoreau built at Walden Pond.

Middle: interior of cabin replica.

Bottom: visitors have long saluted Thoreau by adding to a cairn at the cabin site overlooking Walden Pond.

Facing page: Walden Pond

Another young writer entered Emerson's circle without needing to move to Concord; he was a native of the town. Henry David Thoreau's family lived in several houses in Concord before settling at 255 Main Street. The Thoreau family had a successful pencil manufacturing business. Henry participated off and on throughout his life, making inventive and profitable contributions. After college at Harvard, Henry and his brother John kept a school until John's tragic death from tetanus.

Thoreau became friends with Emerson, who was his senior by fourteen years. Thoreau sometimes lived with the Emerson family, helping with chores and tutoring and entertaining their children.

Thoreau occupied the cabin he built at Walden Pond (on land owned by Emerson) from July 4, 1845, until September 6, 1847. He published *Walden* in 1854 but it was little noticed before his death in 1862. Thoreau felt that Americans were overly concerned with material values, as he expressed in these sentences from *Walden*.

The nation itself, with all its so-called internal improvements, which, by the way, are all external and superficial, is an unwieldy and overgrown establishment, cluttered with furniture, ruined by luxury and heedless expense, by want of calculation and a worthy aim. The only cure for it is in a rigid economy, a simplicity of life and an elevation of purpose.

Orchard House
Above: a watercolor by May Alcott before 1879
Below: Orchard House today

Facing page: the Concord School of Philosophy and Literature

The Alcott family returned to Concord in 1857 and lived in Orchard House for the next twenty years. Bronson Alcott was a stout and energetic abolitionist, always in the thick of the reform movement in his times and town.

Unlike his friends Waldo Emerson and Henry Thoreau, Bronson Alcott is not remembered as an important figure in American literature. He was best known as an educator who respected children as human beings and who rejected corporal punishment. He was appointed superintendent of Concord Schools in 1860.

In 1879, Alcott and his friend Frank Sanborn opened a summer school for adults called the Concord School of Philosophy and Literature. Most of its sessions were held in the unique building pictured at right, which still stands beside Orchard House. Over the next nine years, thoughtful individuals from far and wide came to Concord to participate in this school.

Bronson Alcott in his study at Orchard House.

Sophia Peabody Hawthorne
(1809–1871)

An illustration for *Little Women* by Louisa May Alcott's sister, Abigail May Alcott Nieriker

Facing Page: *Mourning Victory*, the Melvin memorial at Sleepy Hollow Cemetery

Artists

The families of some of Concord's writers included visual artists. Sophia Peabody Hawthorne was a painter and sculptor. One of Louisa May Alcott's sisters, Abigail May Alcott Nieriker, was an artist. She gave early training and encouragement to sculptor Daniel Chester French.

French was born in New Hampshire. His family moved to Concord in 1867, when he was seventeen. Six years later, the Town gave him his first major commission, a statue to commemorate the fight at the bridge. His finished work (see page 1) was unveiled at the centennial ceremony in 1875, which was attended by President U.S. Grant.

The success of *The Minuteman* led to a long career that culminated with French's most famous statue, the seated Abraham Lincoln on the portico of the Lincoln Memorial in Washington, D.C. Several other French sculptures can be seen in Concord. At Sleepy Hollow Cemetery *Mourning Victory* honors three brothers, Asa, John, and Samuel Melvin, sons of Concord, who died during their service in the Union Army in the Civil War. A fourth and youngest brother, James C. Melvin asked French to design this memorial, which was dedicated in 1909. Other works by French are on view at the Concord Free Public Library—see page 22.

Portrait of Elizabeth W. Roberts
by Lucy May Stanton.
Watercolor on ivory
Permanent Collection, Concord Art Association

The John Ball house (1752) was purchased and renovated by Elizabeth W. Roberts for the Concord Art Association, which she founded.

The Concord Art Association is housed in one of the interesting antique houses on Lexington Street. Its 1923 opening was attended by artists including Claude Monet, Robert Henri, Mary Cassatt, and John Singer Sargent. The presence of such distinguished figures was a measure of the influence of the group's founder, Elizabeth Wentworth Roberts (1871-1927), who purchased the house and gave it to the Association. Daniel Chester French was president of its board of directors. Roberts was herself a successful painter whose pictures were widely collected. Some of her paintings were of Concord, including the landscape on the facing page.

Elizabeth Roberts's grandfather made a fortune in railroads and coal. Elsie, as she was called, knew at an early age that she wanted to be a painter. She studied at the Pennsylvania Academy of the Fine Arts, where she received recognition and encouragement. She lived and painted in Europe for nine years, becoming well known for her seascapes and landscapes.

Elsie and her companion Grace Keyes bought a house in Concord, where Grace had grown up—she was a member of the prominent Keyes family. The two lived and traveled together, spending summers on the coast, where Elsie painted many seascapes.

Concord (May)

by Elizabeth W. Roberts, 1919.

Oil on canvas.
Permanent Collection, Concord Art Association.
Gift of Martha Nestor.

Staples Camp in the 1890s

Alfred Hosmer made photographs during the railroad years, before the advent of automobiles, when boating was a popular recreation. Residents of Boston and Cambridge took trolleys or trains to reach canoes stored in waterside boathouses. The Charles River was nearer the city, but the Concord River and its tributaries were also accessible by rail—and less crowded. In these photos Hosmer captured a group of young adults on an outing to Staples Camp, which is at Fairhaven Bay on the Sudbury River. Ruth Robinson Wheeler wrote *Concord: Climate for Freedom* here in 1966. Staples Camp stands today as a unique landmark, surrounded by conservation land, on the federally designated "Wild and Scenic" section of the Sudbury River.

Both Alfred Hosmer photographs courtesy Concord Free Public Library

Two of Concord's notable photographers were inspired by Thoreau. The website of Special Collections of the Concord Free Public Library, which holds many images from both, says this of one of them:

> Alfred Winslow Hosmer (1851-1903) was a lifelong resident of Concord, Massachusetts and a member of one of Concord's oldest families. He made his living as a clerk and later owner of a dry goods store, but also as a photographer. Hosmer was one of Concord's most accomplished early photographers. His images capture the people, houses, institutions, and the landscape of the town, including many locations associated with Thoreau.

The other photographer strongly associated with Thoreau was Herbert Wendell Gleason, who was born in Malden, Massachusetts, in 1855. He was educated for the ministry and served churches in Minneapolis. In 1899, he returned to Massachusetts and began making photographs in Concord. He provided pictures to illustrate editions of Thoreau's *Walden* published by Houghton Mifflin early in the twentieth century. Photographs from his western travels were important in building public support for the national parks. He gave slide lectures on the parks, Thoreau, and New England wildflowers.

Facing page: "Partridge Nest Near Brister's Spring in Concord." from the Robbins-Mills Collection of Herbert Wendell Gleason Photographic Negatives Image II.1908.1. William Munroe Special Collections, Concord Free Public Library.

Concord Free Public Library
as originally constructed in 1873.

The Library's art collection includes a series of dioramas about Concord's history made by Louise Stimson in 1971. This one portrays Henry Thoreau and R.W. Emerson paying a call on Nathaniel Hawthorne, who had been working in his garden. Thoreau has found a stone point—he had a knack for seeing such artifacts.

An excellent place to see artworks pertaining to Concord is the Concord Free Public Library. That's because the founder and lead funder of the library, William Munroe, envisioned it collecting art along with books. The library has remained true to his wish. Of the numerous sculptures on exhibit, French's seated Emerson, which dominates the central room at the front of the library, commands the most attention. In a 1915 article entitled, "A Sculptor's Reminiscences of Emerson," French wrote:

> My statue of Emerson, which is in marble and stands in the Concord Free Public Library, was made two years ago from such materials in the way of photographs and daguerrotypes as could be collected, together with my study of his head [the bust shown on the cover, for which Emerson had sat during his lifetime] as a foundation. It seemed proper to represent him in his prime.
>
> The gown which was used as drapery was one that he wore in his study in the winter and took the name by which it was known in the household, "the Gaberlunzie." It is a heavy, wadded and quilted, dark blue garment, and one can easily believe that its voluminous folds were very grateful to the poet and essayist of a winter's morning in his study in the northwest corner of the house.

Facing page: Seated Ralph Waldo Emerson by Daniel Chester French, 1914, Concord Free Public Library.

Robbins House

Because this book is about Concord's most famous people and events, it does not express the actual social diversity of Concord's history. That limitation can be addressed by visiting the Concord Museum, which tries to represent the complexity of the town's past, and the Robbins House. The Robbins House was built for the descendants of an African American who had been enslaved. The Robbins House website features a downloadable walking tour of African American and antislavery history in Concord.

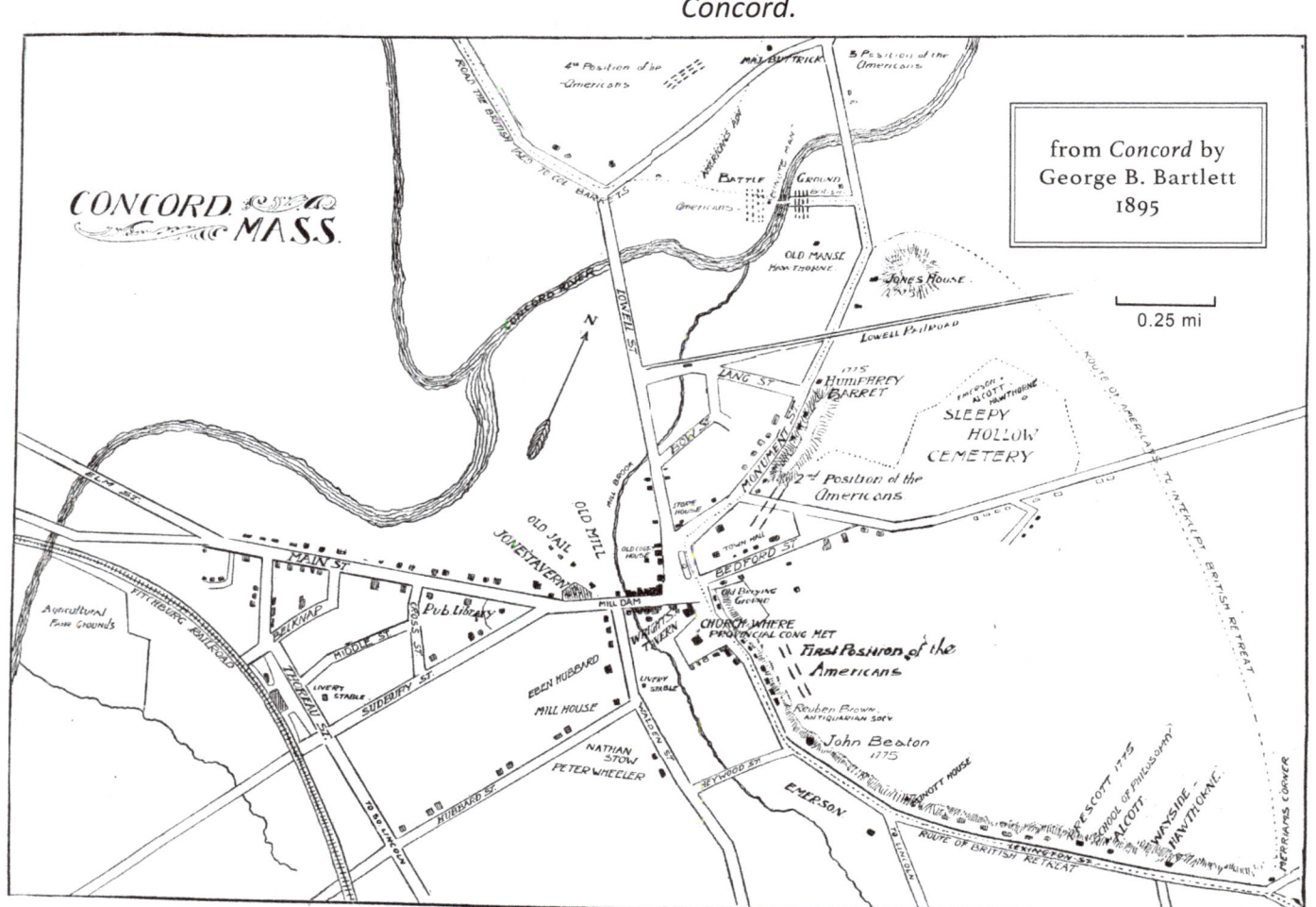

CONCORD MASS.

from *Concord* by George B. Bartlett 1895

0.25 mi

CPSIA information can be obtained
at www.ICGtesting.com
Printed in the USA
JSHW051737280523
39566JS00005B/257